THROUGH THE STORM

THROUGH THE STORM

Copyright © 2018 Courtney Richards

Published by Beyond Expectations Media

ISBN 978-1-912845-12-5 (sc)

ISBN 978-1-912845-13-2 (e)

All rights reserved. No part of this publication may be reproduced, stored in a retrieval system, or be transmitted, in any form, or by any means, mechanical, electronic, photocopying or otherwise without prior written consent of the publisher.

Any people depicted in stock imagery provided by iStockphoto and Unsplash, are models and such images are being used for illustrative purposes only.

All Scripture quotations marked (NKJV) are from the New King James Version of the Bible. Copyright © 1979, 1980, 1982 by Thomas Nelson, Inc. Used by permission. All rights reserved.

All Scripture quotations marked (AMP) are from the Amplified Bible. Old Testament copyright © 1965, 1987 by Zondervan Corporation. The Amplified New Testament copyright © 1954, 1958, 1987 by the Lockman Foundation. Used by permission. All rights reserved.

All Scripture quotations marked (ESV) are from The Holy Bible, English Standard Version. Copyright © 2001 by Crossways Bibles. Used by permission. All rights reserved.

All Scripture quotations marked (NLT) are from the Holy Bible, New Living Translation. Copyright © 1996, 2004. Used by permission of Tyndale House Publishers. All rights reserved.

All Scripture quotations marked (EXB) are from The Expanded Bible, Copyright © 2011 Thomas Nelson Inc. All rights reserved.

Welcome!

Thank you for taking this journey today. I pray your investment of time is richly rewarded as you open your mind to wisdom and revelation truth about your relationships.

This program can eliminate years pain, disappointment and wasted experiences.

Life is always teaching us something. The lessons we learn from the situations of life are entirely based on our individual worldview. Do you live in a friendly or hostile universe? Einstein said the answer to this question is the most important decision you'll ever make.

3 Great Laws

- The Law of Entropy
- The Law of Observation
- The Law of the Seed

These 3 laws when combined together create something quite spectacular.

The Law of Entropy creates the understanding that we've been given delegated dominion & authority (Genesis 1:28) and unless we do something positive, nature (default position of chaos & disorder) will take its course. We have to enforce order. According to Psalm 1:1 (AMP), we are blessed when we choose not to be a passive and inactive bystander in the situations of life.

The way in which we see & perceive things (The Law of Observation) determines our emotions, our expectations and what we ultimately do about situations and circumstances around us; and The Law of the Seed teaches us that we have the ability and power to change our future by what we do with the seed in our possession today. We have the ability to root out bad seeds and plant new ones for a desired harvest.

Understanding and making use of this knowledge with fundamentally transform your relationships.

Ready, Steady, **SHIFT**

Please circle the Y = yes or the N = no, in answer to the following questions.

Ready

There is time in my life to invest in my own development	Y or N
A gap exists between where I want to be and where I am right now	Y or N
I can work on tasks that will help me to develop and grow	Y or N

Willing

I am willing to perform whatever is necessary to reach my goal and aims	Y or N
I am willing to SHIFT in my thinking concerning relationships and marriage	Y or N
I am willing to attempt new ways of achieving my goals	Y or N

Able

I have the commitment I need to succeed	Y or N
I have the support I need to make significant changes to my life	Y or N
I am mentally ready for a different approach to my life	Y or N
I am physically prepared for the encounters I may not have experienced before	Y or N

7-10 Y This program will be effective, exciting and rewarding for you

5-7 Y You may need to make some adjustments before starting this program

1-5 Y You are not interested in SHIFTING!

What do you want to get from this program? ------------------------------------

----

THROUGH THE STORM

Use the notes sections in this workbook to make notes whilst the facilitator takes you through the session.

 Did you know that there are around 250,000 marriages in Britain each year costing around £2.5Bn

No-one gets married expecting to get divorced (unless it's a business arrangement). However, at a ratio of nearly 1 in 2 and costing around £40,000 per couple, there are around 115,000 divorces every year.

OUR AIM

Relating—and the quality of our relationships—is of deep, natural, and inherent concern for all of us and like any human endeavour, takes attention, care, and commitment. This program is designed to help you create a SHIFT in your thinking that supports the building of strong relationships allowing you to flourish whether single or married.

For those that are already married, it could serve as a means of identifying where things may have gone wrong and a platform for making things better.

You'll discover a possibility of being related independent of your past, your expectations, your preferences, or your views—a dimension more powerful than personality or circumstance—a dimension where relationships can become an occasion for creativity, vitality, intimacy, and self-expression.

Marriage Beyond Expectations:

- We offer specialist programs covering various aspects of improving relationships.
- We also offer Mediation/ Conflict Resolution service & Relationship Coaching
- Get in touch on 07957125137 or hello@marriagebeyondexpectations.com
  www.marriagebeyondexpectations.com

Do not be conformed to this world, but be transformed by the renewal of your mind, that by testing you may discern what is the will of God, what is good and acceptable and perfect. Romans 12:2 ESV

Our quest is to wage war on diseased thinking and to embed the divine truth.

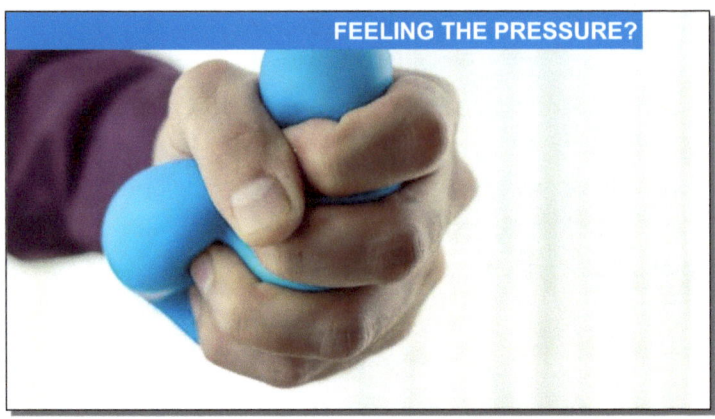

Into each life some rain must fall...

> You've either just gone through, about to go through or are in a storm right now!

We generally start relationships (marriages, friendships, jobs or join churches) with high hopes and expectations for the future.

In marriage we make a promise to each other that in sickness and health, for better or worse, for richer or poorer until death do us part.

In other relationships, like church, we connect with a group or start a ministry because we believe The Lord led us there... and in the case of work, we take a new role expecting things to work out well.

Perhaps you've heard the saying "into each life some rain must fall..." and are thinking to yourself... "what if I'm experiencing more of a deluge? "And what feels like relentless pressure in a storm that just doesn't end?"

In the age of social media, we are used to seeing the beautiful lives of our so-called friends. We often upload our showreel with the highlights of our lives but not the times in the valley – and in the absence of any other information, this often gives a false impression that life is without problems.

The reality is that relationships will encounter times of challenge, problems and storms of life. **You have either just gone through, about to go through or are in a storm right now!**

Issues like ill-health, financial problems, infidelity and bereavement can come and kick you in the stomach, take the wind out of your sails and put relationships under pressure to breaking-point.

During the Christmas / New Year season we tend to use the word "wish" when expressing our sentiments to others. While this is great, when it comes to our relationships, we need to do more than just wish that things will get better - we need to have plans otherwise we'll see the same issues year on year.

But how do you plan for such events in life?

Our thinking plays a central role in how we see and deal with the inevitable storms of pressure. Today, I want to challenge you to think on things that motivates growth in your relationships even in difficult times.

Pressure

- Life, Work & Relationships makes a range of demands on us. These include not only expected tasks and responsibilities but also demands that are unscheduled, inconvenient and often annoying – all of which create pressure.
- From the moment we were born and with our first cry that said hello to this world, 10 Newton's of pressure (gravity) was on our head. Pressure is a fact of life - so we might as well just accept it instead of hoping for a pressure-less life – we therefore need strategies to thrive in our respective environments.

About your relationships and specifically marriage, do you have a plan for the rough times?

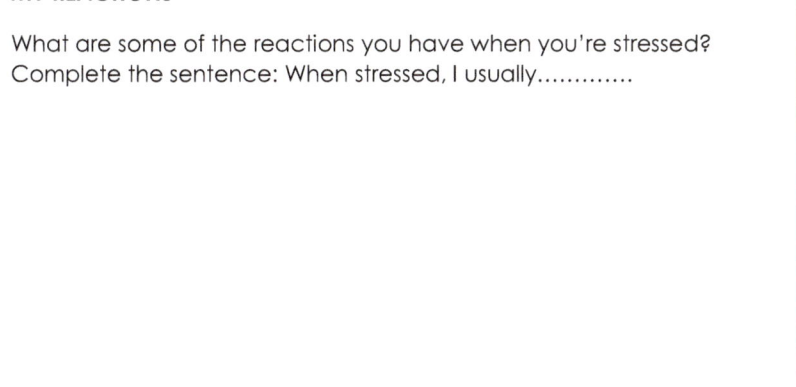

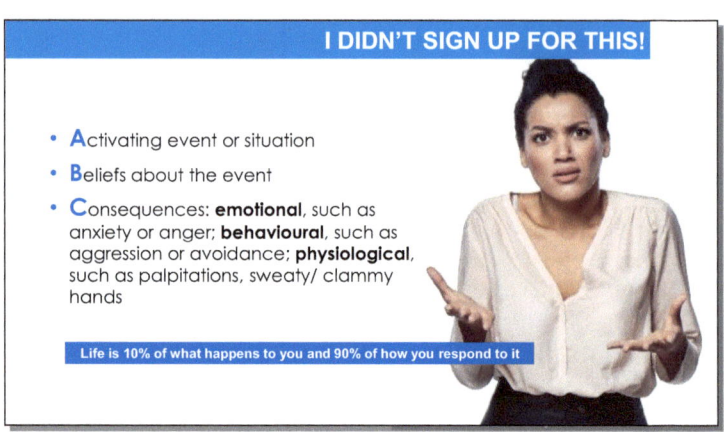

En-route to the fulfilment of your purpose as an individual, couple or work/ministry team; you'll meet opposition internally and externally that will challenge your faith and staying power.

Getting married, or starting any other type of relationship e.g. work or church, we'll have hopes, dreams and aspirations of what will happen in our future and to varying degrees we'd have plans and a picture of the future we're expecting – then stuff happens...

Even though many of us know painful experiences will come and go throughout the course of our lifetime, we often aren't prepared for them as we should be.

More challenging than facing pressure and pain on our own is managing it within a relationship, particularly in a marriage.

Stress is a complex issue and because its linked to our beliefs, no two individuals will be affected in the same way – you see, we all have different ways of dealing with pain and pressure.

STRESS. A common reaction when things happen that are not expected.

Stress and fatigue result when a person's reservoir of personal resilience is drained faster than it is replenished, and when the perceived pressure exceeds our perceived ability to cope.

As stress stems from unresolved or unmanaged pressures, its management is all about equipping yourself with strategies – both mental & physical to cope with these challenges – hence resilience.

The result of pressure is energy production – displayed in one of the following ways:
- Expression – anger, aggression etc
- Repression – anxiety, depression
- Conversion – use it to fuel higher achievement - linked to resilience

As a man thinks so is he...
We are a product of our thoughts. Therefore, our relationships are the products of our combined thoughts.
When going through a storm, your thinking can determine how long the season lasts, how well you come out of it and level of your joy. When you feel as if you're drowning in a sea of problems – many relationships eventually crumble under the mindset of *"I didn't sign up for this!"*

Why me? ☹
Well, why not you? When we experience problems in our lives, it is easy to ask questions like this, and to think that we are being singled out above anyone else – this thinking is unhelpful for you and your relationships.
The temptations in your life are no different from what others experience. And God is faithful. He will not allow the temptation to be more than you can stand. When you are tempted, he will show you a way out so that you can endure. 1 Cor. 10:13 NLT

It's not fair... ☹
When you believe that every should have an equal share in life it leads to wrong thinking when problems occur as your error started when you compared yourself with others. This is unhelpful for the health of your relationships as love isn't a transactional exchange but an independent decision to give **not based** on what another person does.
You need to get used to the fact that there's nothing in creation that's fair.

Good stuff happens to good people – right? ☹

This viewpoint is immature and the recipe for much unhappiness. It follows a very basic view of life that isn't supported in scripture. Just because you love God doesn't mean you are absolved from going through challenges. The key to remember is that rain falls on the just and on the unjust and that he made us more than conquerors – **Romans 8:37**

I must be under a curse 🙁

It's easy to see the difficulties in your marriage or other significant relationships as evidence that you're living under a curse and the sad thing is that many well-meaning leaders have also reinforced that notion.

The devil has 3 principle attributes — killing, stealing & destroying, and all of his actions against us can be put in one of these categories. See **John 10:10**. Any loss sustained as a result of the enemy, can be grouped as loss by invitation (your sin) or loss by encroachment (uninvited intrusion). If an attack has arisen because you have invited the devil in by sin — repent, stop what you were doing and ask God for forgiveness. **1 John1:9**

> *God blesses those who patiently endure testing and temptation. Afterward they will receive the crown of life that God has promised to those who love him.*
> **James 1:12 NLT**

If loss was due to encroachment (trespass against you), you now have every right to file a case against him to God and based on teachings in Exodus and Leviticus, God will not only allow you recompense, there will also be compensatory damages awarded in your favour for your pain and suffering.

The Lord will at times allow the enemy to attack, to set you up for a blessing, so if the situation wasn't caused by your invitation; instead of thinking you've been cursed and are drowning, instead see it as God positioning you to manifest his kingdom. See **Psalm 66:10-12.**

QUESTION TO SELF...

In what areas do you need to change your thinking?

Are you SHIFTING?

For example, I thought……. (old beliefs, I now reject), today I'm moving towards (new beliefs)……

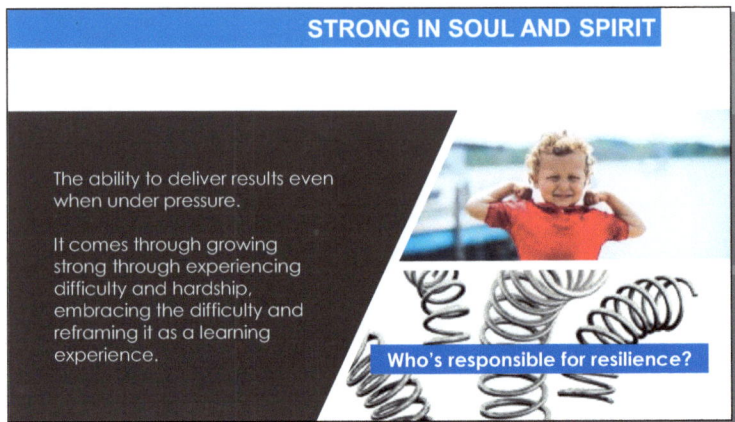

> ear friends, don't be surprised at the fiery trials you are going through, as if something strange were happening to you. **1 Peter 4:12**

When faced with challenging life situation – you can try to move either the issue or the persons involved. However, sometimes it's not possible to move either, so toughening needs to take place so that your marriage or other relationships can withstand the pressure & thrive!

There's a difference between growth and development. Growth relates to something that increases over a period of time – naturally. As long as you've been fed, you will grow all by yourself. Development occurs when pressure is applied. E.g. muscular development comes as a result of pain in the gym.

God often uses pressure to develop a particular characteristic or ability in us. Consider this, where would King David be without Goliath?

Pressure. Necessary for the development of strength in your soul and spirit.

When experiencing pressure in your life that wasn't caused directly by your actions or inactions – know that the Lord won't put more on you than you can bear. See **1 Cor 10:13**

Even if the storm was caused by your actions – when we turn to him, he'll recycle into something good. Consider the story of Samson in the book of Judges.

The bouncebackability (a phrase coined by Iain Dowey – former manager of Crystal Palace FC) refers to the ability to bounce back from bad situations.

- Having a wide range of tools and skills to deal with many different types of challenges.
- Flexibility of thinking – being able to switch between a range of thinking styles to find the best one for the situation.
- The ability to bounce back from difficult situations without suffering lasting damage

Remember! The quality of your relationships is defined by the battles you have won individually and together.

Considering the state of your relationships:

- ✓ How will being resilient benefit your marriage or other significant relationships?
- ✓ Who's responsible for your marriage or other significant relationships becoming resilient?
- ✓ List the changes you're committing to make.

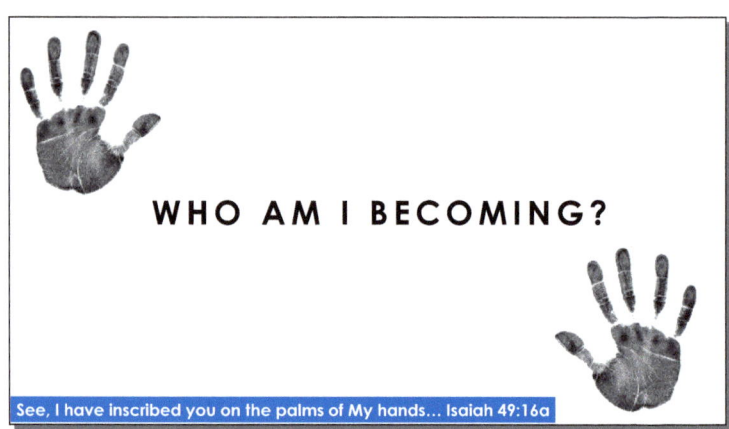

WHO AM I BECOMING?

See, I have inscribed you on the palms of My hands... Isaiah 49:16a

Your journey in God, is less about getting from point A to B (whilst still important), but more about what you become on the journey.

Everything is in a transitional state. We start young, but don't stay that way – nothing actually stays the same. Our marriages and other relationships are no different as we're all in a state of becoming.

But as many as received him, to them gave he power to become the sons of God... John 1:12 KJV

- You cannot rise above your confession. So, what are you saying about yourself and your significant relationships?
- Who are you becoming (Individually and together)?
- Does it line up with the picture that your maker created?
- Are you thriving or just surviving (in a state of decline)? Stagnation is a form of decline too...

Did you know

Pearls are created when a parasite (irritant) enters an oyster. In order to protect itself the oyster releases a chemical which coats the parasite and over time this turns into the beautiful pearl.

Therefore, in this example, the irritation was part of a pre-determined plan. The Lord has planned a life for you before you were even born and engraved you on the palms of his hands (see Isa 49:16, Jer 29:11, Jer 1:5, Ps. 139:16) so, what is your marriage and other relationships becoming?

The Children of Israel's 40yr journey through the wilderness highlighted their intrinsic values that showed a lack of trust in God. The Lord used the circumstances on their journey as a teaching tool until they were ready to enter into the promised land.

Then I went down to the potter's house, and there he was, making something at the wheel. And the vessel that he made of clay was marred in the hand of the potter; so he made it again into another vessel, as it seemed good to the potter to make. **Jer 18:3-4 NKJV**

Sickness and disease, financial problems, infidelity, childlessness, bereavement and shattered dreams etc. can alter the flow and direction of a relationship in ways neither party had initially anticipated or planned for.

As you grapple with coming to terms with a new normal it is easy to find yourself drifting away from each other. The conflict being between the rawness of the emotional pain and turmoil vs. your spirit being alive to God and each other. You want to connect, you want to grow, you want to make things work, you want to get up and try again but the pain just seems all too much.

> MAKE FAILURE YOUR TEACHER, NOT YOUR UNDERTAKER.
> **Zig Ziglar**

The good news is that God made us with emotions and knows that it takes time to work the reverberations of an unplanned situation. The key is to stay in His hands and stay in the relationship – then watch him work on your situation.

Learning to love the life you didn't choose is all about humility and submission. Coming to the realisation that God knows best and that his plan of redemption and reconciliation is never failing – **He always has back up plans.** By submitting to His lead, you'll experience the future and hope that was always planned for you.

- Maintain your connection with God
- Even in the pain, maintain communication with the other party
- Remember, we have a ministry of reconciliation
- God loves creating beauty out of ashes

Are you SHIFTING?

For example, I thought……. (old beliefs, I now reject), today I'm moving towards (new beliefs)……

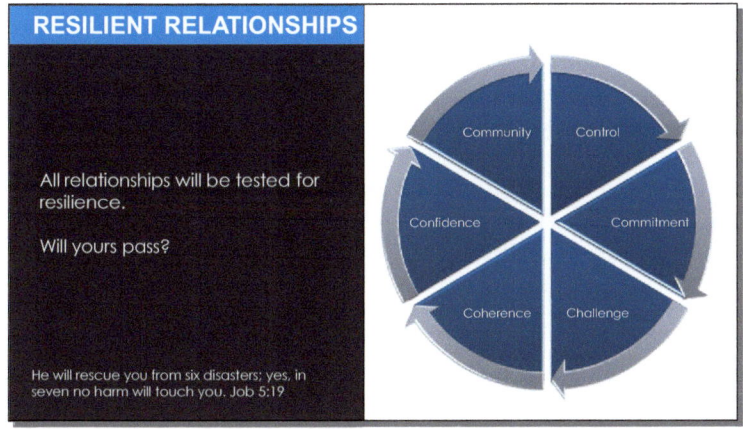

G old, silver or anything precious has to go through a process of evaluation to establish and authenticate its quality. Our relationships are no different, and anything of value will be tested ahead of you receiving the benefits.

Blessed [happy, spiritually prosperous, favoured by God] is the man who is steadfast under trial and perseveres when tempted; for when he has passed the test and been approved, he will receive the [victor's] crown of life which the Lord has promised to those who love Him. **James 1:12 AMP**

Relationships are complex organisms and it's important to recognise and evaluate our individual thinking in the different facets.

1. **Control** – relating to influence
2. **Commitment** – relating to engagement
3. **Challenge** – relating to handling challenges
4. **Coherence** – relating to sound thinking
5. **Confidence** – relating to how we see our abilities
6. **Community** – relating to inter-personal interactions

He will rescue you in six troubles; in seven nothing that is evil [for you] will touch you. **Job 5:19 AMP**

Six is the number of man, and for me this passage means that when situations of man have done their worst (fully tested you), no evil will be able to affect you.

W hat do you have control over?

Inherent in humans is the command to rule and manage our world. See **Genesis 1:26-28**

Internal & External Position of Control

This refers to an individual's perception about the underlying causes of the events in their life. In other words, do you believe that your destiny is controlled by yourself or by external forces?

Individuals with External viewpoint believe that their circumstances are determined by luck, fate or other external circumstances. As a result, they tend to go with the flow and take things as they come but on the flip side often take no responsibility for making changes and can end up feeling like they're been "done to".

Individuals with Internal viewpoint believe they are in total control of everything, seeing the axis of control as within themselves. As a result, they are usually pro-active in dealing with life situations, but on the flip side, panics and tries to control everything when threatened. In marriage this often manifests by the need to control your spouse.

Circle of Concern vs Circle of Influence

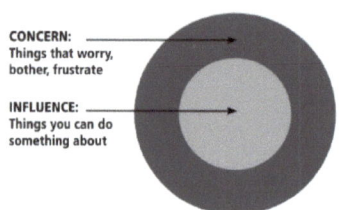

The circle of influence is often smaller than the circle of concern.

There are many things we cannot control, but the more we focus on these things it depletes our energy because we feel stressed, depressed & helpless.

Focus on the things you can do something about and you'll feel yourself getting stronger.

For example, you cannot change your height, but you can choose to wear heels.

Did you know that there are times when God will allow a storm into your life as a development exercise to pull out dormant gifts and unused power & authority? Often, it's only when pressed that we recognise who we really are.

Remember how the LORD your God led you through the wilderness for these forty years, humbling you and testing you to prove your character, and to find out whether or not you would obey his commands. Yes, he humbled you by letting you go hungry and then feeding you with manna, a food previously unknown to you and your ancestors. He did it to teach you that people do not live by bread alone; rather, we live by every word that comes from the mouth of the LORD. **Deut 8:2-3 NLT**

Points to consider:

1. If your happiness is on hold, waiting for someone or something else to change – you're likely to be very unhappy for a long time.
2. Even if you're happy right now, you're also likely to be upset as soon as a situation changes from your cosy world.
3. Make your own choices and do not allow others to choose for you. Own your own happiness.
4. Be proactive.
5. You are not the CEO of the universe – relax, you cannot control everything!
6. You cannot control every circumstance you may face, but you do have control over your responses.
7. You are not in control of your spouse or any other human for that matter! Remember, witchcraft is the desire to control another person for your own benefit.

AREAS TO SHIFT

1. In what ways will your relationships benefit from re-positioning the aspects of control?
2. What changes will you need to make in order to see this benefit?

Loss of employment	Infidelity	Death of child
Rejection from church	Rejection from family or friends	Sickness and disease
Death of spouse	Financial	Abusive behaviour

STORM CATEGORIES

74-95 mph

96-110 mph

111-129 mph

130-156 mph

>157 mph

There are different categories of adverse conditions that can hit your life ranging from the equivalent of a high wind at category 1 to a full blown catastrophic devastation of category 5.

Not all storms are equal, and the impact of a storm will depend on various factors like your age, circumstances, if its happened before, your physical health etc.

It's counter-productive comparing storms with someone else as it will affect each person in a very individual way – quite different from another person.

Some storms last only a short while. Others last years.

- Don't deny your feelings
- Find a way to let emotions out safely
- Forgive yourself & others
- Let go of the need for justice
- Look ahead, not back

Are you SHIFTING?

For example, I thought……. (old beliefs, I now reject), today I'm moving towards (new beliefs)……

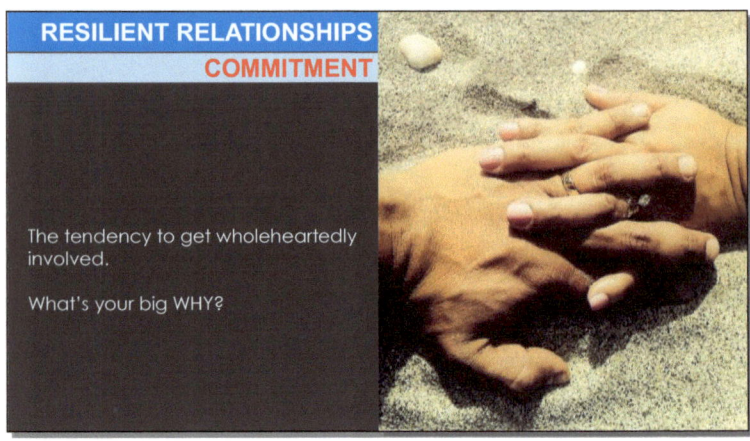

This aspect of resilient relationships relates to your tendency to get stuck in and stay the course through a deep and enduring commitment.

Modern culture teaches that boy meets girl. They fall madly in love and choose to spend the rest of their lives together in wedded bliss.

If we look at biblical culture, individuals would marry for the fulfilment of purpose (obedience to God), out of which love would then grow. Of course, there's an initial attraction that brought you together, but this is not the same as deep love that comes from the type of sacrificial giving mentioned in 1 Corinthians 13. This enduring commitment is rooted in a decision to give, and whether it be in a friendship like biblical characters Jonathan and David or Ruth and Naomi or in a marriage - commitment is huge deal.

This commitment has to go past honeymoon thinking as it's best illustrated when facing a storm of disappointment and emotional pain - commitment will keep you in the game.

Considerations when facing a storm
- Your big WHY – what moved you to get married in the first place? What moved you to start that business, ministry or friendship?
- Re-kindle your passion - studies show that resilient people have a passion or purpose that nourishes and sustains them
- When you go through challenges, resist the urge to cave in and quit
- Sometimes we long for a role/ position - then we get it – then complain all day long about it, when the going gets challenging.
- The best place for solutions is where problems exist – don't be phased by challenges – if you're clear on your BIG WHY – you already have enough inside you to see it through – He's called the Holy Spirit.
- Ask yourself, has God always helped you in the past? If so, what makes you think this time is any different?

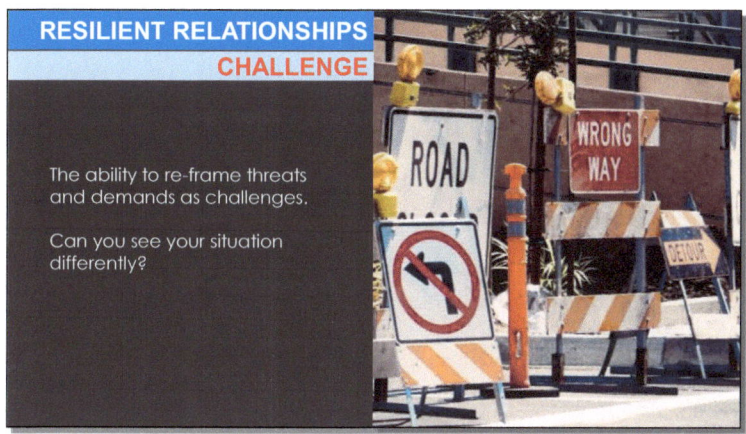

What do you do when you run into opposition, challenges and detours? Find another way.

What I love about the GPS system is that once programmed with your desired address, irrespective of wrong turns – it still works patiently to get you your destination.

Regarding your marriage or other significant relationships, in order to do this, you'll need the ability to see your situation from a different perspective (reframing).

In sport, the best teams are distinguishable by how they act when they don't have the ball – they keep their discipline and never lose their belief in the fulfilment of their goal.

Blessed is the man who trusts in the Lord, and whose hope is the Lord. For he shall be like a tree planted by the waters, which spreads out its roots by the river, and will not fear when heat comes; But its leaf will be green, and will not be anxious in the year of drought, nor will cease from yielding fruit. **Jer 17:7-8 NKJV**

Delay doesn't mean denial

When facing challenges, those engaged in resilient relationships always maintain their divine connection, and in this are connected to the Holy Spirit that leads and guides us into all truth. *You will keep in perfect peace all who trust in you, all whose thoughts are fixed on you! Trust in the Lord always, for the Lord God is the eternal Rock.* **Isa 26:3 NLT**

Those engaged in resilient relationships:
- See situations as a challenge – an opportunity to grow.
- Something to confront & master.

- Are always learning - green and growing, not ripe and rotting.

- Always ask, what can I learn from this situation?
- Recognise that a stress-test beyond that which is needed will always be necessary. A bridge is tested beyond the expected load before it is used.
- Know that pressure produces precious fruit – like a diamond.
- Recognise that their thinking is directly linked to their breakthrough.

In the midst of challenges, by focusing your mind on good things will open you up to receive divine revelation.

Finally, believers, whatever is true, whatever is honourable and worthy of respect, whatever is right and confirmed by God's word, whatever is pure and wholesome, whatever is lovely and brings peace, whatever is admirable and of good repute; if there is any excellence, if there is anything worthy of praise, think continually on these things [centre your mind on them, and implant them in your heart]. **Phil 4:8 AMP**

Making tough decisions
Depending on the storm you're in, you'll need to make some tough decisions that can have life altering consequences. It is therefore important to seek counsel as it is impossible to be objective when under significant pressure and are likely to take the path of least resistance.

You could be looking at moving home, dealing with care of an infirmed loved one etc.

Are you SHIFTING?

Are you now ready to adopt a more powerful position in conflict?

What will this change look like? List the ways below:

When faced with a storm, does your view of life makes sense, add up and is useful?

When under pressure, it is usual for our thinking skills to be impaired – this is because the fight or flight response triggered in our brains suppresses higher level cognitive functions. For this reason, when pressed we'll at times say and do things that actually makes things worse not better and can take us into another storm.

It is said that an answer is servant to a question, so are you ready to check your thinking out? **Can it stand up to critical evaluation?**

High trust relationships benefit as each person is able to challenge the thinking of the other and this leads to better understanding and improvements.

- Is your belief biblically sound? Does it agree with the spirit or letter of the word?
- Is your belief logical? Would a computer programmer agree with your logic?
- Is your belief realistic?
- Is your belief helpful? Where is your belief getting you? Will it help you achieve your goals?

Unrealistic Expectations

An area of thinking errors that'll cause or exacerbate storms is unrealistic expectations. For example:

- Is it realistic or even logical to expect someone that's always been generally messy to suddenly become a picture of organised neatness straight away getting married to a neat person?

- Is it realistic to expect a person who's always been stingy to suddenly become generous after meeting you?
- Is it realistic to expect that your relationship will be the same 10yrs on?
- Is it realistic to expect that your spouse or other's through which you have significant relationships won't make mistakes?
- Is it realistic to expect that you, yourself will never mess up and bring pain to others?
- Is it realistic or helpful to hold to a belief that you won't go through problems?
- Is it helpful to your relationships by holding to a belief that "if you scratch my back I'll scratch yours".

Tell me if this sounds like a prescription for a successful relationship to you:

I have a list of rules. But I'm not going to tell you what they are. If you violate them, I'm allowed to get angry. Also, even though I'm not going to tell you what the rules are, not knowing the rules is also a violation and I'm allowed to get angry at you for that too.

We have things we expect but never make clear. You may be thinking: "But it's obvious. They should know that. I shouldn't have to say it."

The assumption that one's expectations are universal leads to another problem. One partner will believe that the other should know what he or she wants without being asked. This expectation that the mate should be a mind reader is found frequently in distressed marriages.

Other Thinking Errors

TYPE	WHAT IT LOOKS LIKE	CHANGE TO
Blaming	Instead of taking personal responsibility, blaming others for problems that have occurred e.g. *"It's all your fault!"*	Seeing your part in the situation, and working to make things better
All or nothing thinking	Making wild exaggerations e.g. *"I always lose or never make it"*	Using fact-based expressions
Labelling	Rating yourself or others using global statements – e.g. *"I'm a loser"* or *"she's late again. This proves she's incompetent"*	Commenting on specifics skills or deficits.

Magnification	Always blowing things out of proportion	De-magnification, bringing events into perspective
Mind reading	Thinking you know what someone is thinking without firm evidence	Seek to understand
Jumping to conclusions	Jumping to a conclusion without all the information – "You did that on purpose to hurt me"	First finding evidence

Being mindful of your state

When going through a storm, it's important to be aware of your state of mind. In Psalm 51, David prayed about having truth on the inward parts.

- Intention (what are you really trying to achieve?)
- Attention (what are you focusing on?)
- No tension (creating relaxed alertness) – achieved through prayer, taking a breath, doing physical exercise etc.

✓ Being awake to the present moment – not in your past, or future.
✓ Questioning your view of the world – am I generally negative or positive?
✓ Being in touch with what's happening in the now with a non-judgmental view – for example, it's okay to feel angry, disappointed or frustrated as acknowledging where you're currently at prevents you from living in a world of denial.

QUESTIONS TO SELF

On a scale of 1-10 grade your present irritability (1 being peaceful, 10 being you're pulling out your hair)

If you've scored 5 and above, what will you do to turn this around?

If you don't like where you're at, change it. If you can't change it, change the way you look at it.

Are you SHIFTING?

For example, I thought……. (old beliefs, I now reject), today I'm moving towards (new beliefs)……

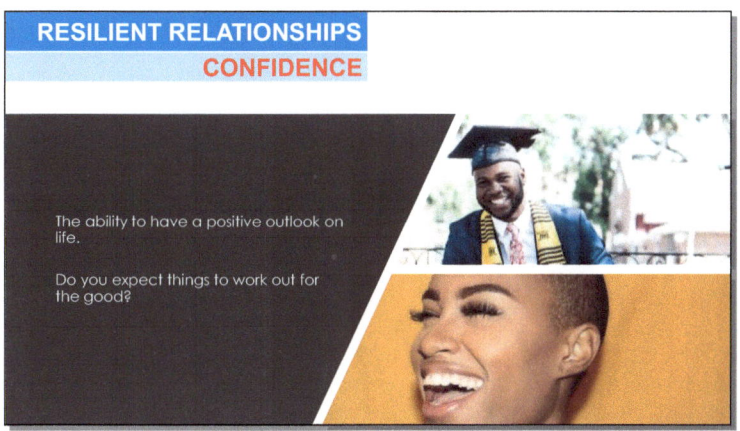

onfidence. The ability to have a positive outlook on life - feeling or showing certainty or self-assurance about something.

I can do all things through Christ who strengthens me. **Phil 4:13 NKJV**
…have no confidence in the flesh. **Phil 3:3 NKJV**
And we know that all things work together for good to those who love God, to those who are the called according to His purpose. **Rom 8:28 NKJV**

Ok, so you've just been hit with a category 4 storm – and you've sustained significant emotional, financial or physical damage. Those who engage in resilient relationships have the knack of being positive and leveraging creative thinking even in the most horrendous of life situations. Creativity is also to see a better end for yourself from where you are today.
They quickly realise that they cannot undo the past, so with the help of the Holy Spirit, their expansive minds create some sweet out of a bitter situation.

> **Despite the storm, do you still expect things to work out well?**

Those engaged in resilient relationships also put no confidence in the flesh. In that they realise that we are all liable to fall and make mistakes (see **James 3:2**). They don't spend their time beating themselves up but dust themselves off, learn the lessons and move forward. They acknowledge that all things work together for their good when following the divine plan.

Horatio Spafford penned the song *"It Is Well With My Soul"* following a family tragedy in which four of his daughters died.

Passing through the Valley of Weeping (Baca), they make it a place of springs
Ps. 84:6 AMP

You may not have chosen to go through the Valley of Weeping, but the resilient make it into a spring (or fountain).

Confidence is linked to your expectation – and what you see is what you get or see in the future. So, what are you expecting from your spouse? What are you expecting from yourself? More of the same…?

Confidence says: I believe I have the ability to do it or can acquire the ability

"For there is hope for a tree, if it is cut down, that it will sprout again, and that its tender shoots will not cease. Though its root may grow old in the earth, and its stump may die in the ground, yet at the scent of water it will bud and bring forth branches like a plant. **Job 14:7-9**

- Those engaged in resilient relationships exude confidence and belief in themselves and each other.
- Encourage each other to go higher.
- Can stand their ground if necessary.

Relationships lacking in confidence

- Have a competitive mindset - making comparisons to others.
- Question God's goodness in their life.
- Often have disappointment and dissatisfaction in what God has given.
- Have the thought that they don't have enough to do what God has asked.
- Often see God as unreasonable and harsh - reaping where he didn't sow.
- Often experience abuse in their relationships

For God has not given us a spirit of fear and timidity, but of power, love, and self-discipline. **2 Tim 1:7 NLT**

QUESTION TO SELF

What changes will you make to increase your confidence?

Those engaged in resilient relationships quickly get to grips with their identity as individuals and as a married unit. They also know how their individual gifts and skills benefit the family, group or team. They also know that eagles fly & live with eagles, meaning that they connected to like-minded individuals.

Love is evidenced by the desire to give without pre-qualifying the worthiness of the recipient. This facet of relationships is underpinned by the notion of sacrificial giving one to another and it flies in the face of reciprocity-based giving – linked to the notion of *"I'll scratch your back if you scratch mine"*.

In a storm, giving isn't about doing what's fair, but what's right.

Are you prepared to give even when you don't see a return? In some cases, for example life altering sickness – you may find the whole dynamic of your relationship changes, where you give more than you ever previously expected.

Sharpening the saw - Getting your edge back
As iron sharpens iron, so a man sharpens the countenance of his friend. **Prov 27:17 NKJV**

After a while of constant giving, we all get tired and lose our edge, and at this point attempting to cut anything with a blunt instrument often does more harm than good. Being connected with others enables you to be sharpened by healthy challenge, stimulating conversations, prayers and encouragement.

A problem shared is a problem halved
Find someone to talk to… Your spouse, a buddy, an accountability partner or someone you can have an honest conversation with.

Thankfulness – the greatest weapon in the storm

ejoice always, pray without ceasing, in everything give thanks; for this is the will of God in Christ Jesus for you. Do not quench the Spirit. **1 Thes 5:16-19 NKJV**

Going through a storm and want to know God's will... here it is!

- Rejoice
- Pray
- Give thanks

This opens you up to get God's perspective on the matter.

I'm not saying it's easy when you've just been kicked where it hurts – it's hard to be thankful. But it's a command!

When you look at the passage below – you may ask yourself, when going through the storm, can I afford not to rejoice, pray and give thanks?

"Because you did not serve the Lord your God with joy and gladness of heart, for the abundance of everything, therefore you shall serve your enemies, whom the Lord will send against you, in hunger, in thirst, in nakedness, and in need of everything; and He will put a yoke of iron on your neck until He has destroyed you. **Deut 28:47-48 NKJV**

> List as many things as comes to mind that you can be thankful for:

Are you SHIFTING?

For example, I thought……. (old beliefs, I now reject), today I'm moving towards (new beliefs)……

To support taking action, below is a checklist for challenging your PIT's (Purpose Inhibiting Thinking).

Am I:
1. Jumping to conclusions?
2. Judging others?
3. Reliant and submitted to God?
4. Giving up at the first sign of trouble?
5. Placing unrealistic expectations on my spouse or myself?
6. Mind reading?
7. Assuming my view is the only possible one?
8. Paying attention only to the negative side of things?
9. Overestimating the chances of disaster?
10. Exaggerating the importance of events?
11. Assuming that I cannot do anything to alter the situation?
12. Expecting myself and others to be perfect?
13. Totally condemning myself (or someone else) on the basis of a single event?
14. Using ultimatum words (must/ should/ have to) in my thinking?
15. Concentrating on my weaknesses and neglecting my strengths?
16. Posing questions that have no answers?
17. Holding bitterness in my heart?

Additional Storm Questions – PET's (Purpose Enhancing Thinking)
1. In what way is the current situation perfect?
2. How could I turn this around immediately, and enjoy the process?
3. What in this situation can you find to be grateful for?
4. What is the value of my current attitude?
5. If my current thinking remained this way for the next 12 months, where will I be?
6. If you were your own coach, what coaching would you give to yourself right now?

What questions do I have?

NOTES

Also available from Beyond Expectations Media

Thinking Fit For Marriage

Built to Last

Making Difference Work

Chaos to Order

Untying Fear Knots

Eye 2 Eye

GYMNASIUM
OF THE MIND